Theory Paper Grade 3 2014 A
Model Answers

1   (10)

2   *There are many ways of completing this question. The specimen completion below would receive full marks.*   (10)

3   (10)

4   (10)

(a)

(b)

5  (10)

6  (10)

7 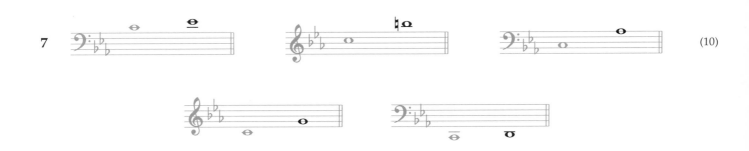 (10)

8 (a)   fast / quick / cheerful / lively (10)
very / extremely
loud
accent / forced / accented
play the notes detached / jumpy / staccato

    (b) (10)

       (i)   simple
                  triple
       (ii)   F

       (iii)

       (iv)

       (v)   demisemiquaver / 32nd note

    (c) (10)

Theory Paper Grade 3 2014 B
Model Answers

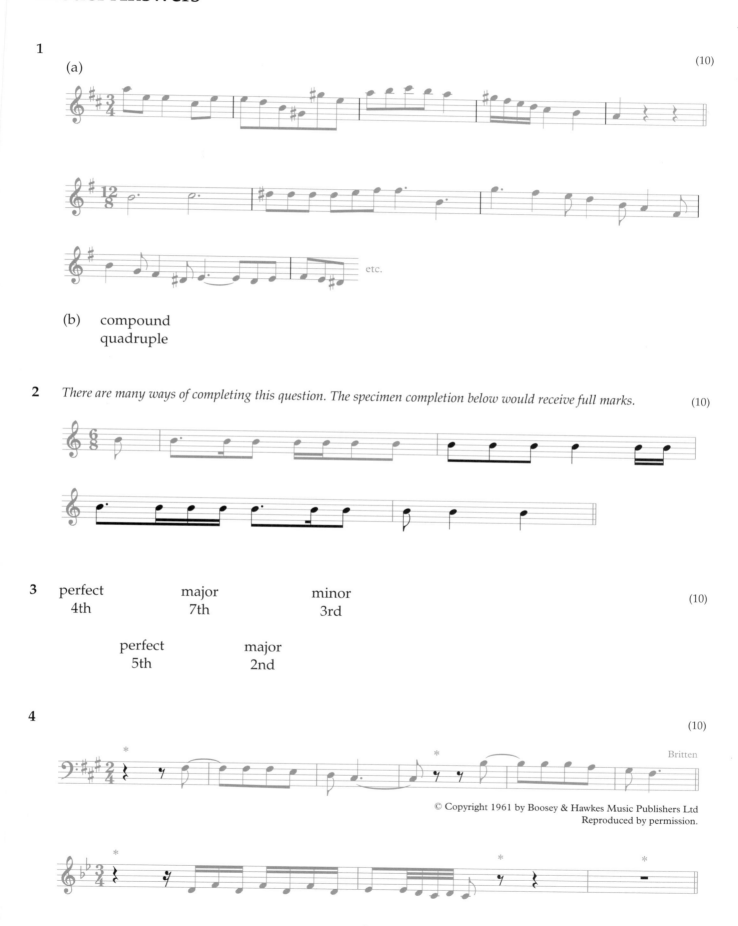

1

(a) (10)

(b) compound
quadruple

2 *There are many ways of completing this question. The specimen completion below would receive full marks.* (10)

3 perfect   major   minor (10)
4th   7th   3rd

perfect   major
5th   2nd

4 (10)

Britten

5 (10)

etc.

6 C harmonic minor (10)
E major
A melodic minor
D major

7 (10)

8 (a) majestic / stately (10)
crotchet beats / quarter-note beats
very loud
with force
getting quieter / gradually getting quieter

(b) (10)

(i)

Andante maestoso

ff con forza

p   *dim.*   *pp*

etc.

(ii) 6

two / two semiquavers / two 16th notes / one quaver / one eighth note

(iii)

p

(iv) demisemiquaver / 32nd note

(c) (10)

or 𝄵

6

Theory Paper   Grade 3   2014   C
Model Answers

1 (10)

2 *There are many ways of completing this question. The specimen completion below would receive full marks.* (10)

3 (10)

(a)

(b)   *There are three possible answers to this question. Any of the answers shown would receive full marks.*

4 (10)

5 G major   C minor   B♭ major   (10)

A major   F minor

6 (10)

7 (10)

8 (a) in the style of a march   (10)

108 crotchets in a minute / 108 quarter notes in a minute /

108 crotchet beats in a minute / 108 quarter-note beats in a minute

very quiet / very soft

accent / forced / accented

hold for the value of both notes / tied notes / tie

(b) (10)

(i) Similarity   melodic shape / intervals of perfect 4ths / rhythm

Difference   pitch / accent in bar 3 / first note of bar 3 has a slur from

previous note / tie on last beat of bar 3

(ii) melodic

(iii) D major

(iv) 6th

(v) false

Britten

(c) (10)

Theory Paper   Grade 3   2014   S
Model Answers

1 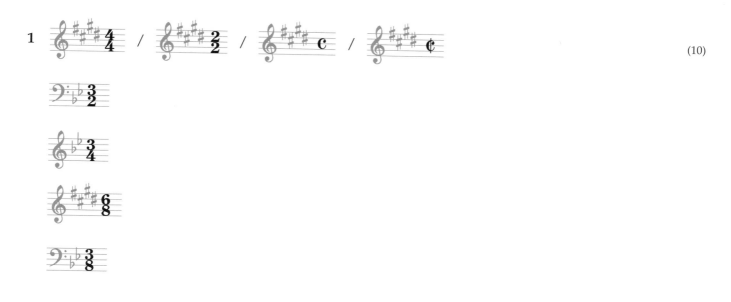   (10)

2   *There are many ways of completing this question. The specimen completion below would receive full marks.*   (10)

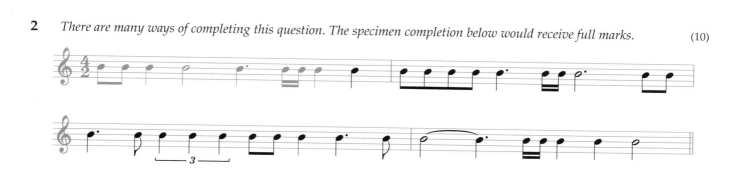

3   (10)

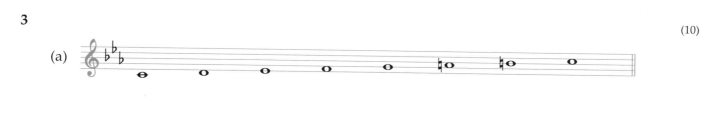

4    etc.   (10)

5   minor   perfect   perfect   (10)
       6th   5th   4th

              major   minor
               3rd   7th

6   B flat   G sharp   F / F natural   (10)
    G / G natural   E flat   C sharp

7   (10)

8   (a)   majestic / stately   (10)
             very / extremely
             104 dotted crotchets in a minute / 104 dotted quarter notes in a minute /
                  104 dotted crotchet beats in a minute / 104 dotted quarter-note beats in a minute
             forced / forcing / accented
             accent / forced / accented

     (b)   (10)
            (i)   3rd
            (ii)   F♯ minor
            (iii) six
            (iv) true
            (v)   compound
                   duple

    (c)   (10)